MY VERY FIRST
BIBLE

ILLUSTRATED BY
DIANA MAYO

WRITTEN BY JAMES HARRISON

DK

London, New York, Munich,
Melbourne, and Delhi

Senior Editor Clare Lister
U.S. Editor John Searcy
Managing Art Editor Diane Thistlethwaite
Managing Editor Linda Esposito
Category Publisher Sue Grabham
Art Director Simon Webb
Production Controller Shivani Pandey
DTP Coordinator Tony Cutting
Religious Consultant Annette Reynolds
Jacket Designer Katy Wall
Jacket Editor Carrie Love

First American Edition, 2005
First published in the United States by DK Publishing, Inc.
375 Hudson Street, New York, New York 10014
Copyright © 2005 Dorling Kindersley Limited
05 06 07 08 09 10 9 8 7 6 5 4 3 2 1

Published in Great Britain by Dorling Kindersley Limited.
A catalog record for this book is available from the Library of Congress.

ISBN 0-7566-0983-6

Color reproduction by Colourscan, Singapore
Printed in Singapore by Star Standard

Discover more at
www.dk.com

Contents

Old Testament

New Testament

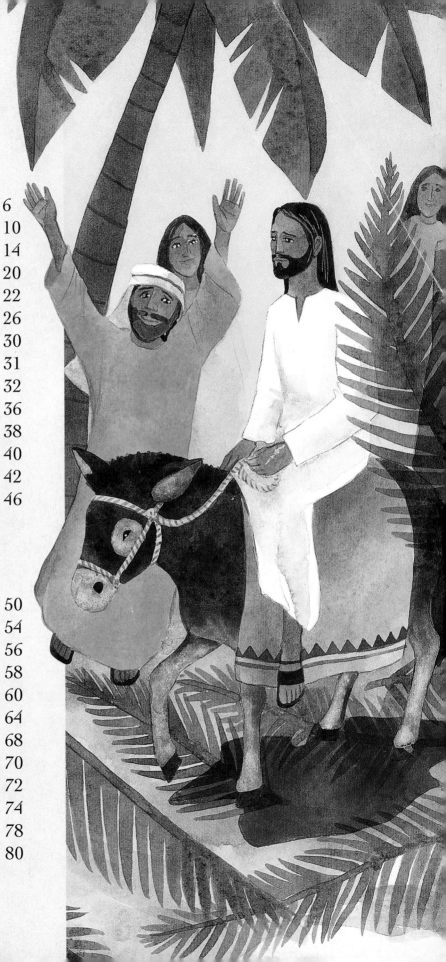

OLD TESTAMENT

God Creates the World

In the very beginning there was nothing at all—
nothing to see, nothing to hear, nothing
to touch. It was black, and cold, and empty.

And God said, "Let there be Light."
And a dazzling light filled the darkness.

Then God created the land,
and the seas, and the sky above.

*"In the beginning God
created the universe."*
GENESIS 1

6

And the earth burst into life
with seed-popping plants
and sweet-smelling flowers—
all budding and blooming
and springing and sprouting.

God made the sun to shine in the
day and the moon to shine at night.

God filled his world
with all kinds of creatures—
all chasing and racing,
grunting and growling,
and roaring and howling.

How many animals can you name?

Then God created man and woman to share his wonderful world and look after it for him.

After six days, God had created the world and everything in it. So on the seventh day he rested.

The Garden of Eden

The first man and first woman were called Adam and Eve. And God loved them.

God put them in a beautiful garden called Eden to enjoy everything he had made.

"Eat whatever you want except the fruit from this tree," said God, showing them a tree in the middle of the garden. "It is not good for you." Adam and Eve agreed.

And for a while everything was perfect.

One day a sneaky snake
slithered up to Eve.

"Why don't you eat that fruit?"
he hissed. "It's deliciousss."
"God told us not to," said Eve.
"That's because he knows it will make
you as smart as him," said the snake.

The fruit did look delicious, so she took
a big bite. Then she gave it to Adam to eat.

As soon as they swallowed the fruit,
Adam and Eve felt awful. They tried
to hide from God, but he found them.

"It was Eve's fault," cried Adam.
"It was the snake's fault," sobbed Eve.
"Don't blame me," hissed the snake
as he slithered away.

God was angry because they had broken
their promise. He sent them out of the garden.

*"The woman saw how beautiful
the tree was and how good its
fruit would be to eat."*
GENESIS 3

Noah's Ark

God felt sad. The beautiful world he had created was full of wicked people. So he decided to sweep away everything in a rushing, gushing flood of water.

Everything except Noah and his family. They were the only good people left in the world.

God told Noah to build an enormous ark with enough room for him and his family, and a male and female of every living creature. "Don't forget to take plenty of food," said God.

14

The sky grew dark and gloomy.

So Noah marched the animals two by two into
the ark—from gangly giraffes and tough tigers
to roly-poly penguins and teeny-weeny spiders.

Then the rains came.

And the rain didn't just pitter and patter; it poured and splattered, and became a terrible flood.

There was ear-cracking thunder and blinding white lightning. So much rain fell that even mountains were covered. Nothing survived except the animals jam-packed onto Noah's watertight boat.

"Noah, his family, and the animals and birds went into the boat to escape the flood."
GENESIS 7

16

But at last the rain stopped,
the waves grew smaller, and the
sun peeked out from behind a cloud.

Unsure if anything else had survived, Noah
released a raven to search for dry land, but
it flew back empty-beaked.

Then Noah sent out a dove, which came
swooping back with an olive branch
in its beak. It had found land.

Can you find the animal pairs?

Safe and sound on solid
ground, the animals spilled
out of the ark.

And God made a dazzling rainbow
in the sky to show his love
for all living things.

Abraham

God told Abraham to go to a new land.
He said, "Pack up your belongings and
I promise that you will be the father of a large family."
So Abraham traveled to the new land
with his wife Sarah and his herds of animals.

One night, Abraham looked up at the twinkling stars—
all shimmering and glimmering, and winking and blinking.

And God said, "Abraham, your family
will be like the stars in the sky—
more than you can count."

Abraham and Sarah thought
they were too old to have children.
But God kept his promise,
and they had a son named Isaac.

"Look at the sky and try to
count the stars; you will have
as many descendants as that."
GENESIS 15

Joseph and His Coat

Isaac's son Jacob had 12 sons. Joseph was his favorite. One day, Jacob gave Joseph a brand new coat. It was as colorful as a rainbow. Next to it, his brothers' coats looked old and drab. They began to hate Joseph.

How many colors can you see?

The brothers were looking after their father's flocks.
As the goats bleated and the sheep went "baa,"
they plotted to get rid of Joseph.

Then, a caravan of camels came by.

The traders were on their way to Egypt with
sweet-smelling perfumes and exotic spices.
"Let's sell Joseph as a slave," said one of the brothers.
So they ripped off his coat and sold him to the traders.

"We'll say a wild animal killed him."
Then, they dipped his torn coat in animal blood
and told their father that Joseph was dead.

Joseph in Egypt

In Egypt, Joseph was sold as a slave. He worked very hard and his master liked him. Then someone told a lie about him and he was thrown in jail. There he met the king's baker and cup-bearer.

"Last night, I dreamed that I squeezed three bunches of grapes into the king's cup," said the cup-bearer. "What could this mean?" "In three days the king will give you back your job," said Joseph.

Then the baker told Joseph his dream:
"I was carrying three baskets of bread to the king
when some birds swooped down and pecked at them."
"I'm sorry," Joseph said. "In three days the king
will have you put to death."

And everything that Joseph said would happen, did.

*"It all happened just
as Joseph had said."*
GENESIS 40

27

The king of Egypt was worried by two dreams.
"I saw seven fat cows grazing by the river, when seven
skinny cows came along and ate them up," said the king.

"In my second dream I saw seven plump ears of corn
growing in a field, when seven shriveled ears of corn
sprouted up and swallowed them."

The king sent for all his wise
men and magicians but no one
could tell him what his dreams
meant. Then, the cup-bearer
remembered Joseph.

"Both dreams mean the same thing," Joseph told
the king. "There will be seven years of good harvest,
followed by seven years of famine."

"Store up grain in the good years to feed the people during the famine." The king was so pleased with Joseph that he put him in charge of Egypt.

The famine spread far and wide.
Joseph's father sent his sons
to Egypt to bring back food.

Joseph's brothers did not recognize him.
"Don't you know your own brother?" asked Joseph.
His brothers were terrified, but Joseph forgave them
and told them to bring his father to Egypt.

Jacob cried with happiness when he saw Joseph.

The Baby Moses

Joseph died in Egypt. His people, the Hebrews, grew in numbers there. The new king did not remember Joseph. He made the Hebrews his slaves. As their number multiplied, the king felt threatened. "Kill all their baby boys," he ordered.

One mother made a plan to save her baby. She made a basket out of river reeds and rushes. Then she put her baby inside and let it float like a tiny boat, hidden in the tall papyrus.

Her daughter Miriam kept watch.

Soon the king's daughter came down to the river to bathe. She found the baby and took him back to the palace. She named him Moses and raised him as her son.

The Burning Bush

Moses grew up in the royal palace, but he was unhappy because his people, the Hebrews, were slaves. He fled the royal palace to herd sheep in another land.

One day, a nearby bush burst into flames. The fire flickered and flashed, but not one leaf fizzled or fried.

Then God spoke: "Tell the king to free my people. You will lead them to a new land."

The Ten Plagues

Moses returned to Egypt and asked the king to free the Hebrews. But the king said no. So God sent down ten plagues on Egypt.

The waters of the Nile turned to blood.

There was a flood of frogs, all slimy and slippery,

annoying gnats that buzzed and bit,

filthy flies,

dead cattle by the cartload,

32

and blistering boils that burst out on people's skin.

Then, heavy hailstones hurtled down,

swarms of locusts gnawed and nibbled,

and a dreadful darkness fell.

Finally, worst of all, every firstborn son perished.

The king gave in and told the Hebrews to go.

"Go to the king and tell him that the Lord says, 'Let my people go, so that they can worship me.'"
EXODUS 8

Moses led the Hebrews out of Egypt.
But when they had gone, the king changed his mind.
He sent soldiers after them to bring them back.

The Hebrews were trapped. Before them
lay the Red Sea, and behind them thundered
six hundred chasing chariots.

And God said to Moses,
"Hold out your staff over the sea."

And Moses did. The waters parted and
the Hebrews hurried across. Then the walls
of water came tumbling down on the trapped
army, crashing and smashing it to pieces.

Can you count the orange striped fish?

The Ten Commandments

Moses and the Hebrews came to Mount Sinai. The people watched as Moses climbed to the top to speak with God.

Suddenly a big black cloud of smoke and fire swallowed up the mountain. Lightning flashed and thunder cracked and echoed all around. The people trembled with fear.

When Moses came down the mountain,
he was carrying two tablets of stone.
Moses held them up to the people,
"God has written down his laws for us."
And the people agreed to live by God's
ten commandments.

Samson and Delilah

The Hebrews settled in Israel, but their troubles were not over. A fierce tribe called the Philistines wanted to throw them out.

Samson was the strongest Hebrew. His strength came from God.

One day, the Philistines visited Samson's friend, Delilah. "We will make you very rich if you find out the secret of Samson's strength," they said. Delilah tried her best to find out. Day after day, she nagged and nagged. Finally, Samson had had enough, and said, "If my hair is cut, I will lose my strength."

Delilah betrayed Samson to the Philistines and they cut off his hair while he was sleeping.

They took him to their temple, and all the Philistines came to laugh at him.

But Samson's hair
was growing.

He pushed against the
temple pillars with all his
might, and the roof came
crashing down on his enemies.

"... and after your son is born, you
must never cut his hair, because
from the day of birth he will be
dedicated to God as a Nazirite."
JUDGES 13

39

David and Goliath

Saul, the first king of Israel, was in trouble. The Philistines had a new champion— a fearsome giant named Goliath.

There was no one brave enough to fight him. Then David, a young shepherd boy, spoke up. "Why are you all so afraid, when we have God on our side?" he asked. "I will fight the giant."

He picked up some stones and took out his shepherd's sling.

When Goliath saw his opponent, he roared with laughter.

David spun the sling above his head and sent a stone whizzing toward the giant.

"The Lord has saved me from lions and bears; he will save me from this Philistine."
I SAMUEL 17

40

Smack!

It hit Goliath right
between the eyes.
And he fell down dead.

The little shepherd
boy became the next
king of Israel.

Jonah and the Big Fish

Nineveh was a big city full of
wicked people. God told
Jonah to go to Nineveh and tell
the people to mend their ways.
But Jonah did not want to.

He boarded a ship going the other
way. That night, God sent a storm.

Lightning flickered and flashed.
Thunder roared and rumbled.
Whirling waves bashed and
smashed the little boat.
"We're all going to drown!"
said the terrified sailors.
"It's my fault," said Jonah. "Throw me
overboard and the storm will stop."

And over he went, splash!
He sank like a stone—

down . . . down . . . deeper and deeper.

Then, suddenly, a big fish swam up
and swallowed him whole.

"But the Lord sent a strong wind on the sea, and the storm was so violent that the ship was in danger of breaking up."
JONAH I

43

Jonah found himself inside the belly of the big fish. For three days and nights Jonah prayed to God. "Give me another chance," he prayed. "I promise I will go to Nineveh."

So the big fish swam to the shore and spat. Out shot Jonah! He landed safe and sound and set off for Nineveh.

What shapes can you find in the picture?

Daniel and the Lions

The king of Babylon sent an army to defeat Israel. Daniel was one of many people taken prisoner.

Daniel worked in the palace. He was very bright and soon became the king's favorite. This made the king's ministers jealous.

They set a trap for Daniel.
They knew he prayed to God,
so they made a law that said
people must only pray to the king.
But Daniel continued praying to God.
So they had him thrown into a lions' den.

All night, the lions that had
roared and clawed
and snapped and snarled . . .
did nothing.

In the morning, the king was overjoyed
to find Daniel unharmed.
"Your God has saved you!" he said.
Then he ordered the jealous ministers
to be thrown into the den.

And the lions tore them to pieces.

"God sent his angels to shut
the mouths of the lions so
that they would not hurt me."
DANIEL 6

47

NEW TESTAMENT

Jesus is Born

The angel Gabriel appeared to Mary. "God has chosen you to be the mother of his child," said the angel. "You shall name him Jesus."

At this time, the Romans ruled over Israel. Mary and her husband Joseph had to travel to Bethlehem for a great counting of the people. When they arrived, Mary was very tired. It was nearly time for her baby to be born.

They could not find anywhere to stay because the town was chock-full of people.

"You will give birth to a son, and you will name him Jesus."
LUKE I

At last, an innkeeper took pity on them.
He let them sleep in his stable.

In a nearby field some shepherds were keeping watch over their sheep. Suddenly, a glittering choir of angels appeared in the sky. The shepherds were terrified.

"Don't be afraid. We bring you happy news," said the angels. "God's son has just been born." The angels told the shepherds to go and worship the newborn king. And the shepherds found baby Jesus in a humble stable, lying in a manger.

What sound does each animal make?

The Visit of the Wise Men

Far away in a distant land, three wise men saw a bright star shining in the sky. "It is a sign that the King of the Jews has been born," they said.

So they traveled to the palace of King Herod in Jerusalem and asked, "Where is the newborn king? We have come to worship him."
King Herod was angry. "I am the king of Israel," he said to himself. But he hid his anger from them. "Find this king so I can worship him too."

The star guided them to Bethlehem, where they found Jesus with Mary. They gave gifts of glittering gold, sweet-smelling frankincense, and soothing myrrh.

" . . . and on their way they saw the same star they had seen in the East. . . . It went ahead of them until it stopped over the place where the child was."
MATTHEW 2

Then they headed home by another
road because God had warned them
in a dream not to go back to Herod.

55

The Hole in the Roof

When Jesus grew up he could do amazing things, such as heal the sick. So people followed him wherever he went.

One day, four men carried their friend on a stretcher to a house that Jesus was visiting. Their friend's legs were paralyzed. But the house was jam-packed with people. They could not even get in the door. So they climbed onto the top of the house, made a hole in the roof, and lowered their friend through it.

Jesus saw them and spoke to
the paralyzed man: "Get up and walk."

The people looked on in wonder as the
man stood up and walked out of the house.

Loaves and Fishes

Jesus chose twelve followers to help him. They were called disciples.

Jesus and his disciples were sitting by the Sea of Galilee. A great crowd of people gathered to hear him speak. As the day wore on, the people grew hungry, but there was nothing to eat.

The disciples looked around, but all they could find were five loaves of bread and two small fish. "How can we feed five thousand people with that?" the disciples asked Jesus.

Jesus blessed the food and started to divide it among the people.

There was enough for everyone.

Everyone ate their fill.
And when the disciples
gathered what was left,
they filled twelve baskets!

" . . . and they all had as
much as they wanted."
JOHN 6

The Good Samaritan

Jesus liked to tell stories that explained the difference between right and wrong. These stories are called parables.

Jesus told this parable to show how we should love and care for people, whoever they are.

A Jewish man was traveling from Jerusalem to Jericho when robbers attacked him. As he lay by the side of the road, a Jewish priest came by, but he did not stop to help. Soon, another Jewish man came by, but again he did not stop.

The wounded man thought he
would die, but then he heard
someone else approaching.

clip-clop
clip-clop

It was a Samaritan on a donkey.
"What bad luck!" thought the wounded man,
because the Samaritans hated the Jews.

61

The Samaritan was a good man.
He wanted to help the wounded Jew.

He poured oil on his bruises. He cleaned his
wounds with wine. And he bandaged his cuts.

Can you find groups of three in the picture?

Then he heaved the helpless man onto his donkey and took him to an inn, where he paid for a room and someone to look after him.

The good Samaritan had acted kindly and done the right thing.

"Love your neighbor as you love yourself."
LUKE 10

The Lost Son

Jesus told this parable to show that even when people do bad things, they can show how sorry they are and be forgiven.

There was once a rich farmer who loved his son very much. But the son wasn't happy on the farm. He wanted to explore the world. "Father, give me money instead of my share of the farm," he said. And so the father did.

The son was very rich
and he had a lot of fun,
but soon he had frittered
away the money.

He was in a
strange land
with no money.
The only job
he could find was
tending pigs.

He was hungry,
dirty, and alone.

After a while, the son came to his senses.
"I would be better off working for my father," he thought.
"He treats his servants better than this."
So he set off for home.

His father saw his son coming and ran to meet him.
"I'm so sorry, Father. I don't deserve to be called your son."

But his father threw his arms around his son and kissed him
"I'm going to throw a big party to celebrate," he said,
"because you were lost and now you are found."

"For this son of mine was dead, but now he is alive; he was lost, but now he has been found."
LUKE 15

Zacchaeus

In Jericho there lived a man named Zacchaeus. Nobody liked him because he was a tax collector for the Romans and because he was very rich.

Zacchaeus heard that Jesus was coming to town and he wanted to see him. But he was so short he could not see past the crowds of people. So he climbed up a fig tree to get a good view.

When Jesus saw him he said,
"Come down from there Zacchaeus.
I want to stay at your house tonight."

The people grumbled: "Why would
Jesus want to stay with that thief?"

But from then on, Zacchaeus was
a changed man. He was kind to everyone
and gave away half his riches to the poor.

*"For Jesus came to seek
and save the lost."*
LUKE 19

69

Jesus Rides into Jerusalem

Jesus and his disciples went to Jerusalem to celebrate a Jewish festival. Jesus rode on a donkey. Crowds came out to welcome him. They cheered and threw cloaks and palm leaves in his path. This was how they greeted a king.

"Jesus is King of the Jews!" they shouted.

"When Jesus entered Jerusalem, the whole city was thrown into an uproar."
MATTHEW 21

The Last Supper

On the evening of the festival, Jesus and his disciples sat down to share a special meal. Jesus said, "This is our last meal together." The disciples felt very sad.

Can you find these things on the table?

They ate bread and drank wine.
Jesus told them to remember him
by sharing bread and wine from then on.

*"When it was the evening,
Jesus and his twelve disciples
sat down to eat."*
MATTHEW 26

The Easter Story

The Jewish leaders were jealous of Jesus.
"How dare he call himself King of the Jews?"
they said. "That's a crime."
They asked the Roman ruler to kill Jesus.

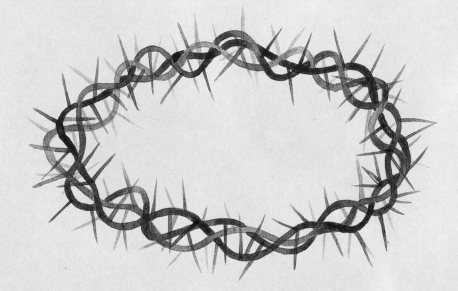

The Romans put a thorny crown on Jesus's head
and nailed him to a cross between two thieves.
His mother and disciples watched and wept.

Jesus asked God to forgive the Jews and Romans.
Then he died. A strange darkness fell,
and the ground shook.

A Roman soldier saw this and said,
"He really is the Son of God!"

Jesus's friends took his body
and placed it in a cool, dark cave.
They blocked the entrance with a big boulder.

The next morning, Mary, a friend of Jesus,
went to the cave. The huge boulder had been rolled
away and the cave was empty. Mary began to cry.

Nearby stood a man.
Mary thought he was the gardener.
"Where's Jesus?" she asked.
When he spoke to her, she realized he was Jesus!

"Tell my disciples that I am alive," said Jesus.
And Mary ran to tell them.

Doubting Thomas

That evening, the disciples gathered together in a house. They locked the doors because they were afraid of the Jews

Suddenly, Jesus appeared.

The disciples were overjoyed to see him. Jesus told his disciples he wanted them to continue his work.

But one disciple was missing. When the other disciples told Thomas what had happened, he did not believe them. "I'll only believe you if I see him with my own eyes," said Thomas.

A week later, all the disciples were together in a locked room when Jesus appeared again.

"Stop doubting and believe," Jesus told Thomas.

Then he said, "Blessed are those who can't see me, yet believe in me."

"Because you have seen me, you have believed; blessed are those who have not seen and yet have believed."
JOHN 20

The Lord's Prayer

Our Father, who art in Heaven,
hallowed be thy name.
Thy kingdom come. Thy will be done,
on Earth as it is in Heaven.
Give us this day our daily bread.
And forgive us our trespasses,
as we forgive those who trespass against us.
And lead us not into temptation,
but deliver us from evil.
For thine is the kingdom, the power,
and the glory, forever and ever.
Amen.